Discovering
YOUR OWN SPACE

Even when you are in a crowded street, you maintain your own personal space around you.

THE SELF-ESTEEM LIBRARY

Discovering
YOUR OWN SPACE

Sandra Lee Smith

THE ROSEN PUBLISHING GROUP, INC.

NEW YORK

To my brother-in-law Mike,
an outstanding young man who has a
special place in my heart.

Published in 1992 by The Rosen Publishing Group, Inc.
29 East 21st Street, New York, NY 10010

First Edition
Copyright 1992 by The Rosen Publishing Group, Inc.

Printed in Hong Kong
Bound in the United States of America

Library of Congress Cataloging-in-Publication Data

Smith, Sandra Lee.
    Discovering your own space /Sandra Lee Smith.
    (The Self-esteem library)
    Includes bibliographical references and index.
    ISBN 0-8239-1279-5
    1. Teenagers—Conduct of life. 2. Personal space—Juvenile
literature. 3. Identity (Psychology)—Juvenile literature.] I. Title.
II. Series.
BF637C5S55 1992
155.9'0835—dc20   91-47516
                                                        CIP
                                                        AC

Contents

Introduction

In a sense, we all fit together in a giant puzzle to make a

complete whole.

Space is the area in which all things exist and where they move. Each person takes up space on this planet. How much space one takes is set by the place where one lives, the city or town, the school, the home, and the body.

Imagine a jigsaw puzzle. Pretend each piece is a person. Each person has his or her own special shape and a space that fits into the picture. When every piece is in place, we have a complete picture.

Take one piece and pretend it is you. There are designs on the piece that give it a special quality different from the others. The other pieces may have the same colors or lines, but they won't be shaded or arranged exactly the same. The way each piece is patterned makes that shape special and unique, just as each person has a special outer appearance. Everyone has a different cell structure and different fingerprints. Hair color, height, and weight are different.

The features of a person may be strong and straight, or they may be rugged and tough. Perhaps they are soft and wispy. They are features and designs that fit you and the way you are inside.

The piece also has a shape. It is unique in that there is no other shape like it in the puzzle. It is separate, yet it fits into the whole. It is a piece that is set apart, yet it belongs in the picture.

The place where that piece belongs is its own special space. No other piece can fit into that place. By the same token, you cannot fit into a space other than your own. You can try to squeeze in, but there will always be a corner or an angle that won't let you fit in.

People also have spaces they fit into best. That is not to say there is only one space for each person, but some spaces fit the outward and inward features of you better than others. If you are happiest playing baseball, you might not fit easily into the space of life of a ballet dancer. If you are outgoing and love parties, you might not easily fit into the space a hermit would like.

Other people may try to fit into your place. Maybe they think your part of the picture looks more interesting than theirs. Maybe that is why you try to fit into someone else's space. When you try, something has to happen; you either break off an arm, bend a corner, or scrunch the piece out of shape. In other words, you have to break your habits, or bend your rules and ethics, or change into a different person. Can you imagine how uncomfortable that would feel?

Some things you try to do in life may not please you or keep you busy enough to make you feel fulfilled. You may end up with too much time or space on your hands. Or perhaps try to do too much and then become stressed or nervous or tired.

Some spaces may be too big, and you end up sliding around, bumping edges on the surrounding pieces. That can be just as uncomfortable as a fit that is too tight.

Let's say some of the pieces do manage to squeeze into the wrong places. Perhaps several small pieces slide into big slots. What happens to the whole picture? Can you see how the misplaced shapes have distorted the scene?

That is what happens to us when we try to fit into a part of society that we are not cut out for. We make a wrong design or shape in the whole picture. It cannot then serve to anyone's good.

Yet sometimes squeezing into new shapes and patterning new designs brings change that is good for the whole picture. Sometimes old spaces are stale and don't serve the good of all, so new pieces need to be molded.

Some changes are not good. Some are good. It is only after the picture is complete and we look back at history that we see how it affects us.

Any change is difficult because of the need to reshape the puzzle. It takes careful planning and

When your family moves into a new home, all of the members must learn to adjust to new personal and mutual spaces.

courage and strength before one commits. To make this kind of change, it is important to know who you are.

Our world is made up of many countries. Each country is a puzzle picture in itself, made up of states or provinces, cities and towns. Each community forms another puzzle picture and is made up of families, schools, and businesses. Each family, school, or business is made up of people. Each person is made up of emotion, will, intellect, body, and spirit.

In a sense, we all fit together in a giant puzzle to make a complete whole. If something happens to one of the pieces, even such a small piece as one person, the picture becomes distorted. That is why it is so important for people to care for one another. We all need to be in good shape to make a sound and whole world.

To understand our role as a piece of the master puzzle, we need to understand our space and where it fits in relation to the whole. Imagine a desert scene. If we are part of the rocky earth, we need to be rugged and tough. If we are a cloud in the sky, our makeup and colors change.

To be in the right place and play our part, we must discover what our space is and how it fits together with the puzzle pieces around us. After all, we want a good and true picture. To do our part in making it so, we need to be sure we are in the right place. We need to do the best things for us, and we must be content to be there. If we can manage that, we will help to make a peaceful and healthy world and a peaceful and healthy self.

Chapter 1

Your Personal Space

Your body is your house, so to speak; the part of the world that is strictly yours.

The body is the space that houses your mind and your spirit. It is the space that is uniquely you. No one will ever have a body exactly like yours. Some family members may look very much like you. Twins can look almost identical. But even twins have their own unique features.

Not only is your body shaped in a special way, it is totally your own space. You can lose a part of your body such as an arm or a leg or an organ. You can also gain replacement parts such as an eye cornea or a heart or a kidney. But you cannot put your mind or your spirit into another body.

11

Your body is your house, so to speak; the part of the world that is strictly yours. No one else can invade the space inside your body unless you allow it.

Our body houses our mind, emotions, and will. Those are strictly controlled by each of us. Other people can influence the way you think and feel. Your home, school, and city can affect the way you think and feel. But no one can think and feel inside your body but you.

Care For Your Body

Since your body is your very own private space, it needs special consideration and care. Without your body to house you on earth, the real you would depart. It is therefore important to consider your body carefully.

The body is like a single piece of a puzzle. We all have the same basic parts: two arms, two legs, a head. Each person, however, has his or her own unique cell structure that makes up the body. Since each body is different, each body is able to do different things. Some bodies are very athletic, and those people are good in sports. Some bodies cannot move easily because they have a handicap. It is important to consider the limits of your own body when you make decisions about what you will do with it.

Because your body is your own private space, you need to be careful about whom you share it with. Most people share space with families. All people share space within a community. You decide, however, how much of your body you will share with others.

Taking good care of your body can give you reason for pride in yourself.

The kinds of foods you eat determine the quality of your body—your special space.

Your body is a big part of your survival, so it should be treated with respect. Since it houses your mind and spirit, it should be considered first when you are making decisions.

In today's world you are faced with many choices that affect your body. You can choose what to put on your body and what to put in it. You decide who will share your body, whether it is a friendly hug or sexual intercourse.

In respect to your body, you must choose wisely so that your special space can be preserved. For example, will you feed your body healthful food full of vitamins and proteins, or will you feed it junk food that has little value? Will you drink fruit juices and water that nourish and cleanse your body, or will you pollute it with soda pop and alcohol? Since it is your own special space in the world, it is to your benefit to take care of it.

Not only must you feed your body well, but you must treat it well. If you want to join in sports, you must eat food high in protein and carbohydrates. You need to exercise daily and build up your muscles and strength. It would be foolish to decide to run a marathon if you have not built up to it. That would cause stress and damage to your body.

If you are a quiet person who likes to read or work on a computer, you would not want to eat the energy-packed foods that the athlete eats. If you did, your body would soon become overweight. You would need to eat less and also be sure to get exercise so that your body and space stayed healthy. A good daily walk not only keeps your body in shape, but releases mental stress as well.

Treating your body with respect also means keeping it clean and properly clothed. You can damage your body with too much sun. Extreme cold without proper clothes can hurt your body. Frostbite can cause you to lose parts of your body.

15

A body needs to be fed and respected and clothed. It also needs to be protected. Fighting or doing dangerous things such as drag racing or diving off a cliff can cause permanent damage. Loud music causes damage to your nervous system and your hearing. Sexual relations can cause the spread of dangerous diseases.

Think Before You Act

It is important to understand the outcome of everything you do. Every person you come in contact with and every activity you engage in could be a threat to your personal space.

Many contacts and activities can be helpful to you. To keep your personal space intact, it is wise to think about what might happen before you decide to hang around with certain people or engage in certain activities.

Remember that your body is your own special space in the world. The decision to share it with someone should be considered carefully. Will the other person give it the same respect and care that you do? Most people are more concerned about their own space than about yours. That sounds cold, but it is true. It is very important to protect your body.

Sexual relationships are the most dangerous threat because they involve intimate contact between your body and another. They also involve your emotions and desires. Not only is it possible for your own body to be hurt, but if pregnancy happens you are involving another life. Sexually transmitted diseases (STDs) can occur as a result of your choices. AIDS is fatal.

When you fall in love you will have to share your personal space.

Sharing your body means sharing your personal space in the world. It should be the most careful choice you make. Each time you share your personal space, you have less to call your own. We all need that special place to which we can retreat to restore our energy, our mind and emotions, and our spirit.

As you grow up, new priorities in your life will lead you to change your concept of your personal space.

Chapter 2

Finding Space Where You Live

All people need a place that they can call their own.

Your body is the space that houses you. Your home is the space that houses your body. Everyone needs shelter to survive, and where you stay to eat and sleep is your home. Most teens live in families. Some live with foster families or other relatives. Some live in institutions, and some live on the streets.

No matter where you live, it is where you first come into contact with others, and it is where you learn to share living space.

Your body needs protection from the weather and from other people. You need a place to sleep where you know no harm will come to you. You need this haven so that your body can rest and restore its energy. You also need a place where you can be alone as well as be loved.

19

If your home does not offer you protection or the basic needs such as food and shelter and love, you may have to take action toward a change. There are services that can help you if your family abuses you. There are services to help you if you are alone or homeless. Churches, temples, the police, school counselors, and teachers can help you find places that are safe to stay.

Watch for Dangerous Moves

Running away from home can provide new space, but it may not be better space. Many teens who are not happy with the space or lack of it at home try to find their own by running off. This can be very dangerous because there are people who take advantage of teens in those situations.

Not having a home or safe place to stay can lead you to take dangerous steps to get one. Some teens join a gang because they think they will be safer. Others get into prostitution and drug dealing seeking a way to live. Still others join the homeless on the streets and end up living in drainage ditches, alleys, or under bridges.

In this country no one needs to live like that. Help is always available. It takes courage sometimes to ask for it. You might be ashamed or afraid to ask for help. But think of what could happen if you don't ask. Many teens wind up in worse situations than they were in at home.

Most teens are fortunate enough to have houses to live in and loving families. Even if you live in a big

Leaving a home where you are not content may lead to a much worse situation.

house and have your own bedroom, you still have to learn to share space. Your family life is the best place to learn those skills.

Rules Make Peaceful Families

Families live together, share meals, help each other when there is sickness, support each other, and offer love. That does not happen without conflict. Sharing space requires each one to give up something for another. Someone may have to concede space to another. To do this without conflict requires great effort on the part of all family members.

For example, if you want to learn to play drums, you need to have a family discussion. You cannot just play any time you like. Others must be considered. A time schedule has to be set up so that the other members know when it is going to be noisy and can plan their own activities accordingly.

If your family has small children or babies, you have to be quiet when you come in late at night. You have to be careful what you leave lying around. If you don't want them playing with your stereo, rules need to be made.

Most families have rules so that the members can share space peacefully. If one member always breaks the rules, there are usually fights and arguments. Breaking the rules causes stress and leaves you with no peace.

Perhaps the family rules are too strict, and you want to assert your rights. Ways of discussing problems need to be set so you can work them out. Otherwise there will be discord in the family.

If problems occur, it helps to have a place where you can go to be alone. There you can cool your temper. Sitting quietly for a while clears your thinking so that you can see a way to resolve whatever is bothering you. This private space where you can go to be alone is a very necessary part of your life.

Most teens need a place to study and do homework. Others need a place to be creative, use their imagination, and think up new ideas. Sometimes you need a place where you can simply rest.

Finding Your Own Place

All people need a place that they can call their own. It is built into us to seek a hangout or home that is ours. If you do not have your own bedroom, you need to find a place that you can claim is only yours. You need a place where you can stay a while with the understanding that no one is to bother you. Little brothers and sisters have to know that you have a right to be by yourself.

Try to find a place that is safe and protected from the weather. A tree house might not be a good place during a rain or snow storm. If your family has a garage, you might be able to make a corner of it into a hideaway.

If you cannot get a whole room, perhaps you can find a corner to make your own. Maybe you could make space under a staircase, or even in a hall closet. Parks, libraries, museums, and churches and temples are places where one can sit alone and be quiet to think and restore the sense of peace.

23

One's own room is a sanctuary where one can be alone to plan and dream about the future.

Even when you are outdoors you can invade the personal space of others by loud noise.

Respect for Others Extends Far and Wide

If you respect the privacy of the others in your family, it is likely that they will respect yours. Much of the way you use space depends on your willingness to get along and care for one another. It is important to learn how to work around space within your family because you will need the same skills in school and the community.

If you do not respect the privacy of others nor consider others who share your living space, there will be discord and unrest around you. Whether you live in a family or an institution, it is important to think about the needs that others have for space just as you need yours.

Friends in school and in the community need the same concern for space. Just as there are rules in the family, there must be rules to allow for space in the school or community.

Sometimes—as in school—your space must be what is assigned to you.

Chapter 3

Living and Working Together

When everyone stays in the spaces set for them, they can move together freely.

In order for many people to live, work, and play together in a place, they have to make rules and codes to live by. In a school, for example, classrooms are usually filled with twenty to forty students. If some sort of order were not set, there would be a riot of pushing and shoving as everyone tried to find their own space.

In cities, spaces are set aside for houses, others for businesses, and others for schools. Every family has a space to live in, and most adults have a space where they work. For all those spaces and people to fit together in a smoothly running society, they need to have rules.

Rules sometimes seem to hinder us. You see signs that say, "Don't do this" and "Don't do that." It seems as if the rules prevent us from having any fun.

Rules, in fact, free us. With rules we can go almost anywhere in the community and feel safe. We know that because the other people will be following the same rules. For example, when you drive down the street, it's a safe bet that all traffic going your way will be on the right side of the road. Traffic going on the left side is coming toward you. All the cars stop at red lights and go with green lights.

When everyone stays in the spaces set for them, they can move together freely. However, if one person drives on the wrong side of the road or does not stop at the red light, what happens? All traffic will stop because of an accident. Some people might be hurt and even killed.

Rules in School

When people do not follow the rules, the community cannot move or work together. When everyone drives in the right space, traffic can flow smoothly and you can go where you want.

Rules in school enable large numbers of students to learn. Time is scheduled and space is set aside where students can go for each class. If a student ignores the schedules, he or she loses out on learning.

The ideal way to learn would be to follow your teacher around in real life, such as on the job or doing the things you need to learn. The way our society has set up education is not like that. There are many more

The cafeteria would be a madhouse if students didn't obey the rules for getting lunch and checking out. These teens also respect each other's space in line.

students than teachers. In order to offer the most education in the smallest amount of space, the school system was designed.

For the system to work, however, all students need to do their part in the space provided. If one student in a classroom acts up and disrupts the class, he or she makes learning difficult for others who are sharing the space.

You may not want to learn, but it is unfair if you disrupt space so that others who do want to learn cannot. A teacher cannot teach if he or she has to cope with a student who is acting up. The system will not allow one person to ruin the chances for twenty to forty others. The disruptive student will soon be expelled from school.

Fitting In on the Job

A business must operate the same way. Workers are given their space with their own job to do. If all do their part and stay in their space, the business runs smoothly. There is harmony and peace as well as production and profit.

If, however, one of the workers intrudes on someone else's space and gets in the way so that the person cannot work, business falters. A boss has to fire a person who cannot operate correctly in a space. The boss cannot afford the loss of production or profits that would cause.

It is important to consider your role in the spaces in your community. If you don't like your role or cannot live with it, you have the option of changing it. In our free society we have set up ways to change rules.

We also have mobility, or the chance to move to a place where we like the rules or the way people are spaced to live.

If you follow set ways for change, there will be less resistance. If you rebel and try to do things your way, society will fight back. That is necessary to preserve peace and harmony.

Before making any decisions about school or work, it is a good idea to look at the space you will be required to function in. If you don't think you can live within the space available, you need to rethink your decisions.

If you decide to go ahead with choices that do not suit the space, you must be prepared for a fight to gain your space in the picture. If you are convinced deep in your heart that the fight is worth the cause, you will probably succeed. However, most people cannot live long in a fight situation. Often they fail, which leaves them with no space to operate in.

If you want success in school or the community, study the spaces available and set your goals toward the ones you can fill. Then you can move forward with peace and harmony.

Yoga and silent meditation are ways of getting in touch with yourself.

Chapter 4

The Realm of Mental Space

Your state of mind makes a big difference in your quality of life.

Your body makes up your personal space in the physical realm. Within your body is your mind, which houses your mental realm. This is the part of you that is truly your own. It is the part of you that controls your body and your space.

It is important to understand how your mind can control your personal space. You can use it for your best interest, or it can do you harm. The way you react to your space determines what kind of life you live.

First you must understand that your soul, which is your mind, emotions, and will, is strictly yours. No one can make you think or react in any way that you don't allow. Parents, friends, school, and television can influence you. You can be talked into things and you can be pressured, but you alone decide how you think and react.

You Are Always in Control

You may think you are controlled by your parents. In a way you are. Your parents have great influence on you. They may insist that you act and behave in certain ways. For example, they may have a rule that you are not to fight with your brother. They can make the rule and enforce it, but it is really you who decides to follow it. You may do so because you would rather not face the punishment your parents may give you. However, you are still the one who decides whether to follow the rule or not.

Your attitude or emotions play a big part in how you handle your space. If you are driving on the highway and a car cuts into your space, you decide how to react. You can pull up close behind and ride his bumper, thus intruding on his space to make him nervous. Or you can put aside your anger and slow down enough to establish another safe space between you and the car ahead.

It is attitude and will that make people act and react the way they do. We learn to control our mind, will, and emotions according to the standards of our culture. We learn to live by the rules of our community because life is easier if we do.

When we don't act or react according to the way society teaches us, we buck the system and end up with a struggle on our hands. Severe differences result in severe action. For example, harming another person's body is not allowed in any culture. Doing so results in criminal punishment and may even result in death.

If we have a problem with the rules, we put ourselves in stress. The inner conflict that results from trying to fit into spaces that our family or culture wants but that we don't want can be very difficult to handle.

Regaining Peace of Mind

Sometimes things happen in our realm of physical space that make it hard to deal with our mental state. If our family has money problems or a loved one is ill, it creates a lot of stress, which in turn affects our body.

It helps to find space to be alone to restore your mental state. Many illnesses could be prevented if people would take time to be quiet in a private physical space and restore their mental space.

Finding a quiet place where you can be alone helps to rebuild your peace of mind. It is also a way to call on and rebuild your spiritual self. Problems and events in physical space are less likely to overpower you if you can keep your mental and spiritual self in order.

Think about times when you are really happy. Maybe it is when your grandparents are visiting you, or maybe you get that after-school job you wanted. Whatever the reason, you feel good. Then at school a friend complains about another friend. Or maybe your boyfriend or girlfriend is mad at you, or perhaps another friend is jealous because you got the job.

When you are happy and feeling up, none of those things really bothers you. However, if you were depressed because you lost the job or your grandparents couldn't come to see you, you might become very angry when you heard the bad news.

Your state of mind makes a big difference in your quality of life. If you can keep your mental and spiritual self at peace, you will improve your physical realm as well. Your reactions will be calm if you are at peace. If not, you may react in anger or violence and thus infringe on someone else's space.

The biggest challenge in dealing with space is to maintain your space without stepping into someone else's space. In large families, institutions, and crowded cities it is especially difficult. That is why you hear people talk about living in the country where it is peaceful. There is peace and quiet because people do have space.

Personal space is something we all need very much. Even in crowds, there are ways to find it. Japan is one of the most crowded places in the world to live. In the streets it is impossible to have much room around you. Even Japanese homes are crowded by our standards. Yet the Japanese people have found ways to maintain their sense of personal space.

The Japanese keep their heads bowed and avoid eye contact. That gives them a sense of being alone within their body even though other bodies may be pressing close to theirs. We do the same thing in a crowded elevator. Everyone faces the door and avoids eye contact with the other people.

A walk in the country or in a park can clear your mind and renew your spirits.

In crowded places people instinctively avoid eye contact to keep from invading the space of others.

Try staring at passengers in an elevator or on a crowded bus. You will see them start to fidget and turn away. It is because you are invading their mental space. You are intruding into their private self.

Different Cultures, Different Spaces

The space needed to maintain that mental self differs in each culture. Watch when you stop to talk to people. You will maintain about the same distance between you and each of them. If it is your boyfriend or girlfriend or a family member, the distance will be less. If it is someone you dislike, it will be greater.

Distances are different in other cultures. Arabs stand much closer than Americans. If an Arab student stops to talk to you, you might become uncomfortable because he or she is so close to you. Their traditional clothing covers the face and head, which gives them a sense of privacy that we don't have in our western clothes.

It is therefore necessary to recognize and maintain personal space. Each of us has a different level of stress. Some can cope with large crowds better than others. Some of us need lots of quiet space. Knowing what space you need and making an effort to achieve it will help you live a more peaceful life.

Family members who share a room learn to make compromises with personal space.

Chapter 5

Goals within the Family

Learning the basic behavior that is allowed within the

space of your community gives you power to control

your space.

When you are aware of the personal space you require, you then need to begin to set it up. The place to start is in your home. When you have found a place that is yours, you need to convince your family of your needs.

Most of the time we try to settle these matters peacefully. Having family talks, appealing to parents or whoever is in charge, explaining your reasons all can help. Force is the last resort. Throwing a brother or sister out of your room instead of working out a deal only leads to further problems.

Look at your goals and your personal needs. Take into account how much space you need, and then try to obtain it. When you approach the problem reasonably and in a calm spirit, you can begin to work out a way that will give you what you need without infringing on the rights of others.

Being reasonable means that you may not have everything your way. As in big business deals, you need to learn to bargain. For example, if you want to play loud music, you need to find space where it won't offend others. If your parents won't permit it in the house, you might seek another place such as a park.

Have you really solved the problem? Not if there are people who are enjoying the park. You may be easing your parents' ears, but you are intruding your music into the space of other people who may not want to hear it. Not only that, loud music is dangerous to people's health, including yours. It interferes with space in a way that can't be blocked out.

If your loud music is hurting people's ears and bodies, if it is interfering with other people's privacy, you might need to decide to play it at a moderate level. Is loud music worth the hassle with parents and neighbors?

Your values must come into the decision when you are dealing with issues that involve others. You must decide whether to focus on your self-interest or put the needs of others before your own.

Most successful people and contented people have learned to give and take when it comes to sharing

Your band can practice in the basement—if other family members are not disturbed.

Touching other people without their consent is an intrusion on their space.

space. Your home is the training ground. Your parents or adult relatives give you the culture standards designed to help you fit into your community.

Learning the basic behavior that is allowed within the space of your community gives you power to control your space. You can look at what you need as a person and see how that will fit into what is there in your world.

Invasion of Your Mental Space

Sometimes space is not controlled. If your physical space is intruded upon, it can affect your mind, but only if you let it. For example, if you are walking down the hall at school and someone shoves you, that person has invaded your private space. The invasion has not yet intruded upon your mind. Only your body has been pushed. If you walk on as if nothing has happened, it is forgotten and your mental space is not invaded.

But if you let the push interrupt your train of thought, you have allowed it to invade your mind. If you stop walking and let anger rise up, or if you confront the person who shoved you, you have allowed the invasion to intrude on your mental state.

Notice the word *allowed*. You had no control over the physical shove. It happened before you could stop it. You do have control over the mental invasion. The reaction of your emotions, mind, and will determines how much your mental space is affected.

Rape is another invasion of the physical realm. It is deeper than just the space around you. It is an actual invasion of your body.

Yet no matter how many times a victim's body is assaulted, there is no way anyone can touch his or her mind or spirit. Those are touched only if the victim allows them to be. If the victim can shut out thoughts of it and go on with life, the assault cannot invade his or her mental and spiritual space.

However, if the victim keeps remembering and reliving the assault, or harbors thoughts of revenge or hatred, the victim has allowed the rape to invade his or her mental space as well.

With regard to serious invasions such as war, violence, rape, child abuse, or tragic accidents, it is very difficult to keep such things from invading your mind. Often a person goes into shock. That is a protective device of the body to keep the mind and spirit safe.

Sense of Love and Values

When the crisis is over and the shock wears off, the painful event will try to invade your mind and heart. That is when you need to be strong and hold your values, your ethics, and your spiritual beliefs close to you. They will help to ward off the invasion.

People who have a strong sense of love and values do better in stressful situations. If those elements are lacking in your life, it would be a benefit to you to seek them from some valid source. Family is the best place to start. If they are not to be found there, ask school counselors, religious leaders, or friends who have these strengths.

Looking for love and inner strength among friends who are as lost as you are will not help. Sharing problems can help sometimes, but more often than not the other person's problems become yours and you are both still suffering. Find someone who is mentally and spiritually strong.

For the same reason, looking to cults or gangs or other negative forces for a sense of belonging cannot work to your good. At some point their troubles will become yours. Your mind will be invaded as well as your spirit.

Friends, relatives, and leaders who are strong give you the hope and will to keep your mental space free from the clutter of tension, stress, fear, and worry that can so quickly bring you down. Focus your thoughts on the things around you that are good and honest. Find relationships that offer love and encouragement. These things will keep you strong.

Volunteer work can help to define a teenager's interests and goals.

Chapter 6

Your Place in the World

To decide what space you will occupy in the picture of

your whole community, you need to examine your goals

and interests.

    As teens, most of your time is spent in the school system. Some of you have jobs and are therefore in the workforce. Others are active in temple or church, social clubs, or sports. All of these activities involve time and space.

    Most communities in the United States offer a wide choice of activities. Therefore each person needs to decide the space in which he or she wishes to move around.

    Remember the picture puzzle? It helps to see the whole picture, the cover of the box, to decide in what area a piece should go. If you have a blue piece for a desert scene, it is a good guess that it is part of the sky and fits at the top of the puzzle.

If you are male you will fit into certain parts of the society without any problem. Likewise, if you are female there are other parts of society you will fit into easily. Most parts of society accept both males and females. For example, a temple or church will have both males and females, but the woman's mission will have only females. The recreation program has both male and female sports players, but only males can play on the men's volleyball team.

Identifying Your Goals

To decide what space you will occupy in the picture of your whole community, you need to examine your goals and interests. What do you want to do with your life? Are you interested in sports, carpentry, social services, the fire department, sales and management? Your interests will determine what space you need.

Students going to college will want to find space in the school and public library. The classes they choose will be those needed for entrance into a college or university. The friends they share space with will be those who share their interests.

If you intend to work in your father's garage, it is likely you will choose the garage to hang around in. Your friends will probably be interested in cars. The courses you select in school will be those that will help you in auto mechanics.

Conflict happens when you are not sure about who you are or what your goals are. You may wander into space that doesn't suit you. For example, if you don't know what you want to do after you graduate from high school, you may not have any activities to look forward to. People who know what they want to do find activities that relate to their goals. If you want to work with cars, you'll find plenty of things to do around a garage. If you hope to enter one of the health professions, you can help a lot and learn a lot by volunteering at a hospital or a nursing home.

People who do not know for sure what they want can easily be misled into activities they don't really fit into. Say, for example, it's a rainy afternoon and you're bored. Some friends call and invite you over to smoke some dope. Such an invitation might be appealing if you do not have your goals set and know where in the picture you want to fit.

Other sources of conflict arise when people try to fit into a space in which they don't belong. They have their goals set and know what they want, but can't quite squeeze into that space. Girls who want to play sports that have included only men are a good example. Girls can fight and tough it out until they force themselves into the slot, but those who break the new ground will not find the fit easy to handle.

The nice thing about a live puzzle picture such as a community or school is that the picture can shift and change. The first girl on a men's baseball team had to squeeze into a space that didn't fit her. Over the years, and as more females have worked their way into the area of sports, there are now places into which they can fit. The picture has changed to meet the needs and demands of society.

Choosing Your Special Space

You must look at all the spaces available and decide whether to slip into one that fits easily or to push and struggle to get into another space. This can be a negative move or a positive move. A lot depends upon your reason for the decision.

Negative moves are decisions to move into space into which you don't morally fit. It may be inviting to decide to hang around a crowd that parties with drugs and sex. You may think you fit into this space, but later you will discover that your health is failing, as well as your grades and your relationships with family and friends.

Positive moves are decisions to move into space into which you fit both morally and by inclination, space in which you can do well and enjoy yourself. If studying is easy for you, it will be easy to take college-bound courses. If studying is difficult, you can try to fit into the program but it will be difficult. Your success in fitting will depend on your motive.

If sports come easily to you, you will be able to fit into a sports program. If sports do not come easily, taking on a sport could be difficult. If you sing well, your space might easily be a choir. If you try to join a choir and can't sing, you will have difficulty fitting into that space.

Nothing is wrong with trying to fit into spaces that are not for you. Many great heroes and heroines in our culture overcame great odds to do that. You have to be willing to do the pushing and squeezing. If you are not that driven to seek a certain space, it might be

High school is a good time to explore various interests and occupations.

wise to look around and find what places you could enjoy.

If you can't decide or don't seem to find a pattern you fit into, talk to your school counselor. He or she has many tests and tools that can help you see the direction you would probably enjoy the most. Then you can explore the areas in which you have high aptitude and perhaps find a hobby or occupation you will enjoy.

Your Space Must Fit into the Picture

Remember that what you do find must fit into the whole picture. Remember the puzzle of the desert? You cannot bring in a piece from another puzzle such as a jungle scene and expect it to fit into the desert. The space you decide to take must fit into the school or the community. If you like hard rock music and go to the park to play it very loud, you not only take space that does not fit into the scene of a quiet park, but you ruin other people's space.

Part of fitting in is making the picture complete. Fitting in will be to your advantage and also to the advantage of the community. The choir does not benefit if you can't sing. The volleyball team does not benefit if you can't play. If you insist on playing anyway, the spot on the team will bring strife, not the pleasure you want out of your activities.

Choosing to belong to a gang or rob stores is harmful to the community. It is like trying to place a puzzle piece from another puzzle. Disruptive behavior in school or in the street does the same thing. It might bring you satisfaction for the moment, but because you are harmful to the whole society you will be taken out or put away.

The community or school cannot allow itself to be ruined by a piece that doesn't belong. You cannot allow yourself to be beaten by trying to fit into a space where you don't belong.

Look carefully at your values, your goals, your needs, and your desires. Look at your physical body and what space in the community you fit into. When you have a clear picture, you can set the action to fit into your special role in life. Set your goals and begin to fulfill them. Then you will be on the road to peaceful and prosperous space.

Glossary

adrenaline Hormones made by the body.

AIDS (acquired immune deficiency syndrome) Fatal infection of the body's disease-fighting immune system.

aptitude Suitability.

carbohydrates Chemical compounds that include sugars and starches.

commitment The pledging of oneself to a cause or plan.

community A body of people living in the same place under the same laws.

conflict A struggle or fight, especially a long one.

disruption Disorder, or breaking apart.

distortion Act of twisting out of shape.

harmony Internal calm.

imagination The ability to form mental images of things not really present.

institution Public society or corporation; e.g., a school, juvenile hall, prison, church.

invade To enter for war; to enter or force oneself upon another's property or rights.

marathon Long-distance race.

privacy The state of being apart from others.

prostitution Offering one's body for sexual purposes for pay.

protein Food source providing essential amino acids.

spirit The essence of life

STDs (sexually transmitted diseases) Any one of numerous diseases that are acquired by sexual activity.

stress Physical or mental pressure.

unique Being the only one.

For Further Reading

Fiction

Ames, Mildred. *The Silver Link, The Silken Tie.* New York: Charles Scribner's Sons, 1984.

Cole, Brock. *The Goats.* New York: Farrar, Strauss, Giroux, 1987.

Crutcher, Chris. *The Crazy Horse Electric Game.* New York: Greenwillow Books, 1987.

Crutcher, Chris. *Running Loose.* New York: Greenwillow Books, 1983.

Crutcher, Chris. *Stotar!* New York: Greenwillow Books, 1986.

Greene, Bette. *Summer of My German Soldier.* New York: Dial Press, 1973.

Hinton, S.E. *Tex.* New York: Delacorte Press, 1979.

Sachs, Marilyn. *Thunderbird.* New York: E.P. Dutton, 1985.

Wersba, Barbara. *The Carnival in My Mind.* New York: Harper & Row, 1982.

Wersba, Barbara. *Crazy Vanilla.* New York: Harper & Row, 1986.

Nonfiction

Baldwin, Dorothy. *Health and Friends.* Vero Beach: Rourke Enterprises, 1987.

Buckalew, M.W. Jr. *Learning to Control Stress.* New York: Rosen Publishing Group, 1982.

Cohen, Daniel. *Meditation: What It Can Do for You.* New York: Dodd, Mead & Co., 1977.

Goldberg, Lazer. *Learning to Choose.* New York: Charles Scribner & Sons, 1976.

Goodbody, Slim. *The Force Inside You.* New York: Coward-McCann, Inc., 1983.

Klein, David. *How Do You Know It's True?* New York: Charles Scribner's Sons, 1984.

Margulies, Alice. *Compassion.* New York: Rosen Publishing Group, 1990.

Schleifer, Jay. *Citizenship.* New York: Rosen Publishing Group, 1990.

Smith, Sandra Lee. *Coping with Decision-Making.* New York: Rosen Publishing Group, 1989.

Smith, Sandra Lee. *The Value of Self-Control.* New York: Rosen Publishing Group, 1991.

Thomas, Alicia. *Self-Esteem.* New York: Rosen Publishing Group, 1991.

Index

About the Author:

Sandra Lee Smith has taught grades from kindergarten through college level in California and Arizona.

As a consultant in connection with Arizona State University, where she obtained her M.A. in Bilingual/Multicultural Education, she has conducted workshops for teachers and parents throughout the Southwest.

Ms. Smith has been hired as a consultant by the Central Valley Teacher Education Center in California and the Bureau of Indian Affairs in New Mexico to teach aspects of the whole language process.

Active on legislative committees and in community projects, she has helped design programs to involve parents in the education process.

In response to the President's Report, *A Nation at Risk,* Ms. Smith participated in a project involving Arizona State University, Phoenix Elementary School District, and an inner-city community in Phoenix. Participants in the project developed a holistic approach to education that Ms. Smith and others successfully implemented in their classrooms; from their research and application, a whole language program emerged involving the three C's—Composition, Comprehension, and Critical Thinking.

Photo credits:

Cover photo: Stuart Rabinowitz.
All photographs by Dru Nadler.

Design and production by Blackbirch Graphics, Inc.